THE DONNINGT

by
Colin Handy

Cotswold Walks Between Donnington Brewery Inns

REARDON & SON

CHELTENHAM, ENGLAND

Published by
REARDON & SON
Publishers
56 Upper Norwood Street, Leckhampton,
CHELTENHAM, GLOS GL53 ODU

Copyright © 1991
REARDON & SON

Fully Revised
Third Edition 2003

Written, researched and photographed
by
Colin Handy

Maps and illustrations
by Peter T. Reardon
Special thanks to Hilary Allison for the
original typing and 1997 revisions

ISBN 1 874192 00 6

Printed by
STOATE & BISHOP (PRINTERS) LTD
Cheltenham, Gloucestershire

INTRODUCTION

The Donnington Way

Donnington Brewery brews real ale in the very heart of the Cotswolds and maintain 15 public houses in what must be one of the country's most perfect areas. For many, the name of Donnington means more than good beer, it is a whole way of life.

Now, for the first time, the pleasure that is Donnington is opened to the rambler in the form of a 62 mile walk appropriately called "The Donnington Way".

It is possible to join the circular walk at any point of your choice but in order to allow you to leave a vehicle, the walk starts and ends in the ancient Market Place at Stow-on-the-Wold.

Most Donnington houses offer bed and breakfast facilities, enabling you to walk distances of your choice. Almost 90 per cent of The Donnington Way is in Gloucestershire, although the walk passes through the counties of Worcestershire, Warwickshire and Oxfordshire.

All the rights of way listed have been walked to establish their existence on the ground, following wherever possible public footpaths and bridleways. Careful planning will ensure that you are able to enjoy a traditional welcome in each Inn.

To help you walk the way maps have been drawn for each walk, but if you would like greater detail then we advise obtaining O.S. Maps 150, 151 and 163.

The Donnington Way is a true Cotswold delight for the rambler who thrives on well-kept countryside and hidden villages. The charm of rural Gloucestershire is treasured by every serious walker and The Donnington Way now offers an opportunity for that treasure chest to be open to all.

Colin Handy.
Cheltenham, 1997.

THE COUNTRY CODE

* Guard against all risk of fire

* Fasten all gates

* Keep dogs under proper control

* Avoid damaging fences, hedges and walls

* Keep to paths across farmland

* Leave no litter

* Safeguard water supplies

* Protect wildlife, wild plants and trees

* Go carefully on country roads

* Respect the life of the countryside

Waymarking colour code:
* Blue Arrows - bridleway
* Yellow Arrows - footpaths only

WHEREVER YOU ROAM IN THE COUNTRY, FOLLOW THE CODE!

The Queen's Head Inn, Stow-on-the-Wold to
The Coach and Horses Inn, Longborough

Distance 2³/₄ miles

For the convenience of long term parking your walk starts and ends in The Square, Stow-on-the-Wold. Stow is regarded as a focal point for the North Cotswolds, lying 700 feet above sea level and having eight major routes radiating from its centre. The Town Square is filled with picture postcard houses and shops and remains busy throughout the changing seasons. Prominent among the mellow stone buildings is your starting point, the majestic Queen's Head Inn, an Inn of old world charm.

This, the first of the 15 Donnington Public Houses is typical of the style of their establishments, retaining as it does a real country pub atmosphere in two bars full of character. Tradition seems to be the cornerstone for Donnington's success and The Queen's Head plays its part by offering traditional farmhouse cooking to be enjoyed over traditional pub games, such as Shove Halfpenny.

The pub is busy the year round but especially so during Cheltenham's Gold Cup Festival Week in March each year. As a tribute to its dedication to the comfort of racegoers, the Inn has been voted "Best Pub" on the Cotswolds by the writers of "The Sporting Life".

Leaving the Queen's Head, turn left and head down High Street, passing the Police Station on your left, and make your way to the busy A429. Turn right and walk out of town on the A road towards Moreton-in-Marsh crossing over after the traffic lights.

After a quarter of a mile, just past the Broadwell turning, there is a layby on your left and an entrance to a new house called "The Paddocks". Here, leave the road and start out on a bridleway taking you to the village of Donnington. It was in this pretty little hamlet that the remaining forces of the Royalist troops surrendered to the Parliamentarians on March 21 1646, which was to be the final defeat of the bitter English Civil War in Gloucestershire.

At the end of the bridleway, bear right onto an unclassified road. Pass a telephone kiosk on your left and as the road sweeps right, bear left. After a further 100 yards pick up a footpath sign taking you to Longborough. As you leave Donnington village you pass close to a farm on your right. Pass around the barn, turn left and keep the fence on your left and go straight ahead over two small fields before once again picking up a bridleway, (marked with a blue arrow) taking you into the bottom right-hand corner of the field.

The bridleway is now well marked and well defined and takes you all the way into the village of Longborough, which is a pure delight with two small shops and a cluster of neat cottages. Keep right and make your way to its green and Cross and your first stop, The Coach and Horses Inn.

This compact, cosy Inn offers a traditional welcome in a true village style. Its location is such that to look out from the beer garden will transport you back 100 years. The Cross, the cottages and the Church lend themselves to be captured on film.

The medieval Church, with its 13th century tower, is steeped in history and has many interesting features, including gargoyles, burial monuments and a richly sculptured font. It is well worth taking time out to visit.

Longborough village is visited several times each year by a touring band of Gloucestershire Morris Men, encouraged by Donnington Brewery.

4

STOW on the WOLD to LONGBOROUGH

The Church of St James

Longborough

The Coach and Horses Inn

To Ganborough

Love Walk

Wood Pigeon

Ox-Eye Daisy – Seen in fields during Summer

Donnington Manor Farm

Donnington

Telephone kiosk

Stow on the Wold.
The Lantern headed Town Cross,
standing in the Square since the
14th century, was restored 100
years ago in memory of
Sir Joseph Chamberlain who
donated to the installation
of an up-to-date water supply
in the town.

A 429 To Moreton in Marsh

To Broadwell

To Evesham   A 424

B 4077
To Broadway

Police Station

The Queen's Head   Stocks

St Edward's Church   St Edward's Hall

B 4068   Stow on the Wold
To Andoversford

A 436 To Chipping Norton

A 429 To Northleach and Cirencester

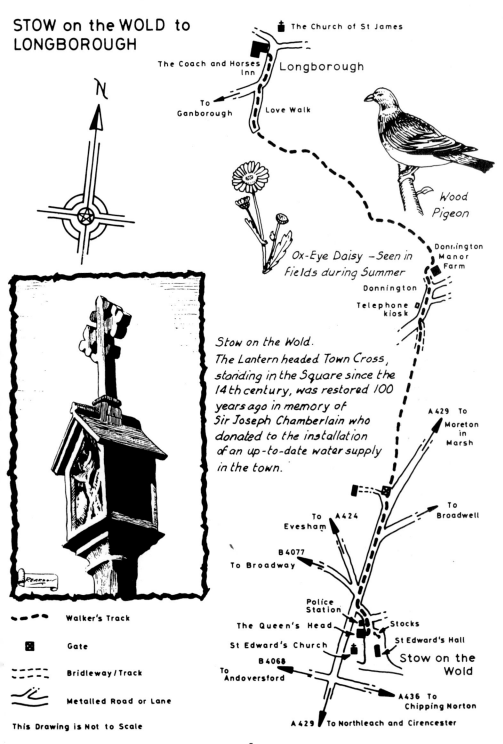

●━ ● ●   Walker's Track

▣   Gate

▭ ▭ ▭   Bridleway / Track

〰   Metalled Road or Lane

This Drawing is Not to Scale

The Coach and Horses Inn, Longborough to
The Coach and Horses Inn, Ganborough

A short steep climb now awaits you as you go from one Coach and Horses direct to another Inn of the same name.

As you leave the Longborough Coach and Horses, turn left and climb out of the village towards the A424. Half way up the steep climb, a memorial bench offers a quick resting place and a magnificent view out over Warwickshire and Gloucestershire.

Finish the climb to a Y junction and bear left. This short length of road now takes you direct to the busy A road. Take great care in crossing the road and turn left. Follow the road for about 200 yards and the second building on your right is the next Coach and Horses Inn.

This typical English Inn is built entirely of local stone and was originally two cottages and stables. More than 250 years old, the Inn is a popular eating place and even features a select park for Caravan Club members. It prides itself on its extensive menu and throughout the year its car park is filled with visitors' vehicles. Whole families are used to the hospitality on offer and children are particularly welcome. Winter walkers get a bonus welcome with a real log fire to enjoy the Donnington beers by on a frosty day.

A view of the Cross and St James Church from in front of the Coach and Horses Inn at Longborough.

LONGBOROUGH to GANBOROUGH

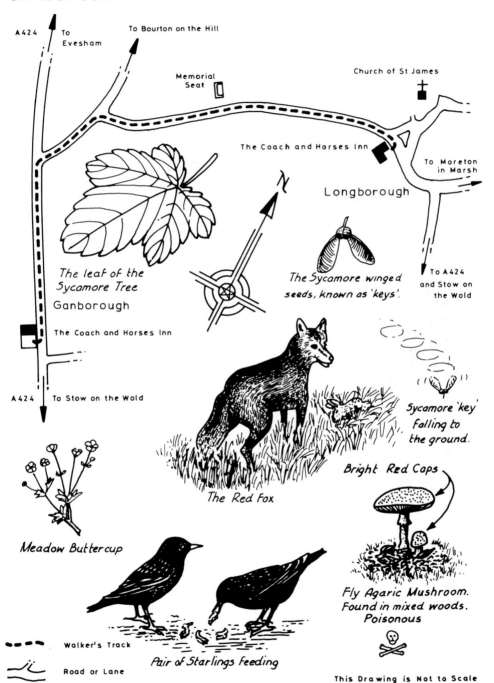

A424

To Evesham

To Bourton on the Hill

Memorial Seat

Church of St James

The Coach and Horses Inn

Longborough

To Moreton in Marsh

To A424 and Stow on the Wold

N

The leaf of the Sycamore Tree

The Sycamore winged seeds, known as 'keys'.

Ganborough

The Coach and Horses Inn

A424

To Stow on the Wold

Sycamore 'key' falling to the ground.

The Red Fox

Bright Red Caps

Meadow Buttercup

Fly Agaric Mushroom. Found in mixed woods. Poisonous

Pair of Starlings feeding

●●● Walker's Track

Road or Lane

This Drawing is Not to Scale

The Queens Head Inn, Stow on the Wold.

The Coach and Horses Inn, Longborough.

The Coach and Horses Inn, Ganborough.

The Coach and Horses Inn, Ganborough to
The Golden Ball Inn, Lower Swell
(via Donnington Brewery)

Distance 3$^1/_2$ miles

Leave the Coach and Horses Inn and once again cross the busy A424, turn right and then immediately left down a minor metalled road back to the village of Longborough. You will soon recognise your original point of arrival in the village where you turn right for the bridleway that you left earlier.

At the end of Love Walk and the start of the bridleway, look closely to your right and you will find a well marked footpath which you should now follow. After three fields, with some farm buildings ahead of you the footpath divides three ways. Take the path going right, through a wooded passage which takes you back to the A424. Cross straight over onto an unclassified road marked Condicote. Turn left at the first junction marked Upper Swell.

Very soon you arrive at the 'Mecca" itself –the famous Donnington Brewery. The mill buildings which house the Brewery have been used in various ways for seven centuries, although they have been converted and rebuilt several times. In 1827 the buildings were bought by the present owners, the Arkell family, who started a brewery here in 1865. The family also farmed the surrounding fields, producing barley for their brewing process, but today the hops come from Worcestershire and the malt from Norfolk. The mill remains in good working order and its wheel is still used to drive machinery.

The beautiful Cotswold buildings that form the Brewery stand in an idyllic position, surrounded by lawns and paths which in turn lead to the millpond. Unfortunately, the brewing process does not lend itself to spectators and as a result cannot be thrown open to visitors. However, a fine view is obtained from the minor road as you pass by on your way to the B4077.

At the junction with the B road turn left and walk through the village of Upper Swell. The village boasts a fine Tudor manor house with a two storeyed porch alongside a small church, complete with a Norman doorway.

Just before a narrow bridge over the River Dikler, a well-marked footpath goes into the right, which now takes you across three fields and down a metalled road on the Abbotswood Estate to the village of Lower Swell.

The estate boasts a fine 20th century house built by Sir Edwin Lutyens and was once the home of tractor millionaire, Harry Ferguson.

As you leave the estate, turn right on the B4068 road which takes you direct to your next destination, The Golden Ball Inn, around which, to all intents and purposes, the village of Lower Swell is built.

The Golden Ball offers a fine range of food and beers and a very warm welcome. The building dates from the 17th century and has been licenced for more than 100 years. Again, the Cotswold stone and exposed beams are a delight to the eye. A unique feature of this Inn between April and September each year is the opportunity to watch or join the traditional garden game of "Aunt Sally". The Golden Ball has a local league team playing this game, which requires competitors to throw "sticks" at an "Aunt Sally" doll to score points.

The village church has several Norman features and is worthy of a visit before pressing on.

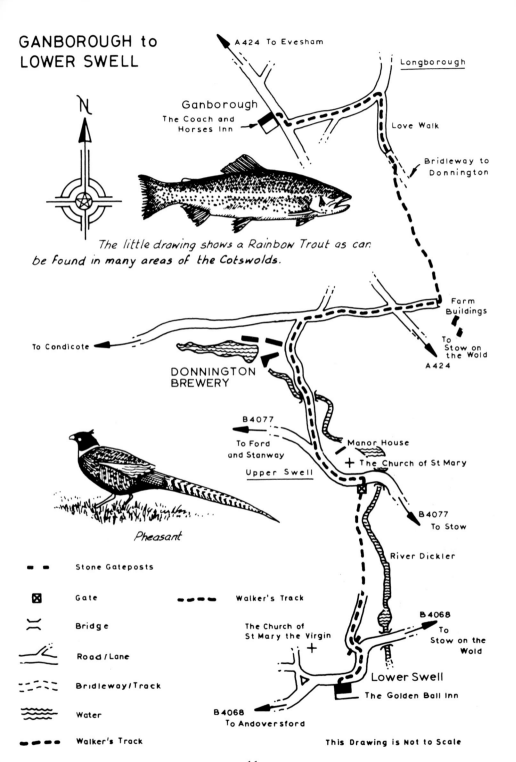

GANBOROUGH to LOWER SWELL

N

A424 To Evesham

Longborough

Ganborough
The Coach and
Horses Inn

Love Walk

Bridleway to
Donnington

The little drawing shows a Rainbow Trout as can
be found in many areas of the Cotswolds.

Farm
Buildings

To Condicote

To
Stow on
the Wold

A424

DONNINGTON
BREWERY

B4077

To Ford
and Stanway

Manor House

The Church of St Mary

Upper Swell

B4077
To Stow

River Dickler

Pheasant

B4068
To
Stow on
the Wold

The Church of
St Mary the Virgin

Lower Swell
The Golden Ball Inn

B4068
To Andoversford

This Drawing is Not to Scale

Stone Gateposts	
Gate	
Bridge	
Road / Lane	
Bridleway / Track	
Water	
Walker's Track	

Walker's Track

11

The Golden Ball Inn, Lower Swell to
The Fox Inn, Great Barrington.   Distance 9 miles

From the Golden Ball, turn right onto the B4068 and immediately right again to follow the road that loops around to the right to rejoin a minor road in the heart of the village. Turn left and walk up the road.

As you leave the village, also leave the road by taking the well-marked bridleway on your left. The path takes you over several fields to the attractive Hyde Mill and continues on the bridleway to a metalled service road and the busy junction of the A424 and the A429.

Taking great care, turn right and walk along the A429 towards Cirencester for about 300 yards. Just past The Fosse Manor Hotel, cross over to a layby and follow the footpath sign into the field, heading off at a right angle. The path passes through farm buildings at Heath Hill and continues South for three more fields before it joins an unclassified road where you turn left.

It is now time to savour the walk as it passes right through the pretty village of Wyck Rissington. Continue past the ancient church, with its massive squat Norman tower and well-tended churchyard. After another 150 yards, when the road sweeps left, carry straight on a track marked with a "No Through Road" sign.

Follow the track for a quarter of a mile where it peters out at the crossing of a bridleway. Turn left and after 20 yards turn right to follow a footpath sign taking you straight ahead across the field. In the second field bear slightly left heading for St. Peter's Church at Little Rissington, which you should now head for. The church dates from the 12th century and is set apart from the present village by a field where the original village lay prior to the Black Death in 1347. An unusual feature of its graveyard is a small "Military Cemetery" for 75 servicemen who died while stationed at RAF Little Rissington. These include airmen from Canada, Australia, New Zealand and America. The West window of the church is dedicated to their memory and includes a stained glass "Red Arrow" as a tribute to the squadron which was once stationed there.

From the church, walk up into the village and cross the main road into Pound Lane. The lane loops around left before rejoining the main road at the entrance to Manor Farm. On your right is a well-marked bridleway which you should now follow over several fields to the village of Great Rissington. The bridleway is virtually straight the whole way. However, at one point it joins a farm track. As the track sweeps left be sure to continue straight ahead on the bridleway, always keeping the hedge on your right.

You enter the village with a farm on your left and should walk straight ahead. As the main road sweeps left continue straight ahead on the road marked "Unsuitable for Heavy Goods Vehicles". Go down the hill and start to climb the other side. Opposite "Rosemary Cottage" turn left up a small spur road. Turn left again and almost immediately right. This road soon turns into a dirt track. Go straight on for a third of a mile. Just after a large farm barn the track is marked as a bridleway. Keep straight ahead.

The well-used bridleway now runs for 1½ miles, dipping into a valley and rising again, before emerging onto the road for Great Barrington, where you turn right. Here, you keep the estate wall of Barrington Park on your right as you follow it for a further third of a mile. Barrington Park contains a grand Palladian mansion originally built for Earl Talbot, which unfortunately is not visible from the road, but its herds of grazing deer are.

You pass the village church as you walk by the estate and this is worthy of a visit as its many fine features include a delightfully sculptured memorial to Mary, Countess Talbot, by the famous 18th century sculptor, Joseph Nollekens.

LOWER SWELL to GREAT BARRINGTON

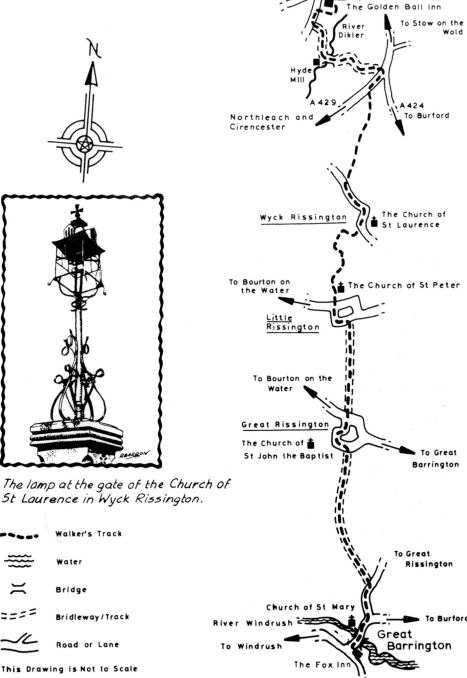

Lower Swell

The Church of St Mary the virgin

The Golden Ball Inn

River Dikler

To Stow on the Wold

Hyde Mill

A 429

A 424
To Burford

Northleach and Cirencester

Wyck Rissington

The Church of St Laurence

To Bourton on the Water

The Church of St Peter

Little Rissington

To Bourton on the Water

Great Rissington

The Church of St John the Baptist

To Great Barrington

To Great Rissington

To Burford

Church of St Mary

River Windrush

To Windrush

Great Barrington

The Fox Inn

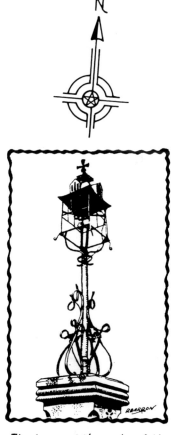

The lamp at the gate of the Church of St Laurence in Wyck Rissington.

- •‑•‑•‑• Walker's Track
- ～～～ Water
- ≍ Bridge
- ==== Bridleway / Track
- ～⌇ Road or Lane

This Drawing is Not to Scale

Continue on down the road to your next port of call, The Fox Inn. In truth, the Inn lies equidistant between Great Barrington and Little Barrington alongside the picturesque River Windrush. Originally a Coaching Inn, the converted coach house now houses an alley for Long Skittles.

Offering bed and breakfast for up to nine people, The Fox Inn prides itself on being a real English pub in the true sense of the word, totally unspoilt by time. Visitors can participate in a whole range of pub games while enjoying good food and beers or just sit and watch the River Windrush run by.

LITTLE RISSINGTON — GLOUCESTERSHIRE.

— THE PICTURESQUE COTSWOLD VILLAGE of LOWER SWELL, in GLOUCESTERSHIRE —

The Golden Ball Inn, Lower Swell.

The Fox Inn, Great Barrington.

The Fox Inn, Great Barrington to
The Black Horse Inn, Naunton.

Distance 10^1/$_4$ miles

Leave The Fox Inn and take the minor road towards Windrush. After approximately ½ mile and just before the first farmhouse on your left, look for a stone stile in the hedgerow on your right.

Climb the stile onto a footpath which runs straight across the field to your left. Make for the right hand side of the large farm ahead of you. Go over another stone stile, keeping the farm and dry stone wall on your left. Cross a small brook and at the top of the rise, the path divides. Take the path going to your right, cross a farm track and continue straight ahead towards Sherborne. The walk in the Windrush Valley is quite superb.

As you enter the hamlet of Sherborne between small cottages, you meet a metalled road where you turn to your right. Follow this road uphill for just over a mile and at the top, where the road sweeps gradually left, look for a Yellow Arrowed footpath sign into a field on your right. Enter the field and turn left onto the footpath.

The path follows the hedgerow and emerges alongside the stables of Broadmoor Farm and bears left up to a metalled road. Turn right and walk through the farm complex. Pass the old farmhouse on your right and after 50 yards turn left onto a footpath taking you down through three fields to the fast flowing River Windrush at New Bridge.

Now turn left on this little-used road. After approximately 300 yards, take a well-marked bridleway to your right. Keep straight ahead to pass Lower Marsh Farm where you meet a metalled road which becomes easy walking all the way into Bourton-on-the-Water. Look out for a road sign along this lane which was obviously erected by someone with a sense of humour. It points across the fields and gives its distance in "as the crow flies miles".

When you meet the major road, turn left and follow the River Windrush through the tourist delights of Bourton-on-the-Water, including the Model Village, an exact replica of the village in Cotswold stone, Birdland, with its collection of exotic birds, a Model Railway and a well-stocked Motor Museum.

Your walk through Bourton, following the river, brings you to the junction with the A429 which you should cross straight over, with great care. Continue to follow the river on your left using a well-used bridleway with Blue Arrowed markings. The path now takes you away from the river and after two fields zig-zags through a wooded copse. Here, the bridleway splits and you need to continue on the path going off to your left.

The path soon becomes a road and drops down through a small splendid mill before climbing again. At the top of the climb turn right with the road and pass straight through the neat buildings of Aston Farm. The well-marked route passes between the farm's enormous sheds and out again into open fields before entering a wood.

Unfortunately, the wooded section you now follow can get extremely muddy but you will soon discover the worth of this route when you eventually emerge in a fine valley which is fertile, green and lush. It is a magical section full of sheep and unusual cattle, pheasants and partridges.

When the footpath meets a metalled road the signing is confusing but your path lies straight ahead and you should follow the valley for a further half mile. Where the path divides, cross the stream on a stone bridge and follow the Blue Arrowed route up the steep climb at a left angle. At the stile go straight on.

Now cross carefully through the fairways of the Naunton Downs golf course on a well marked path, looking out for stray balls.

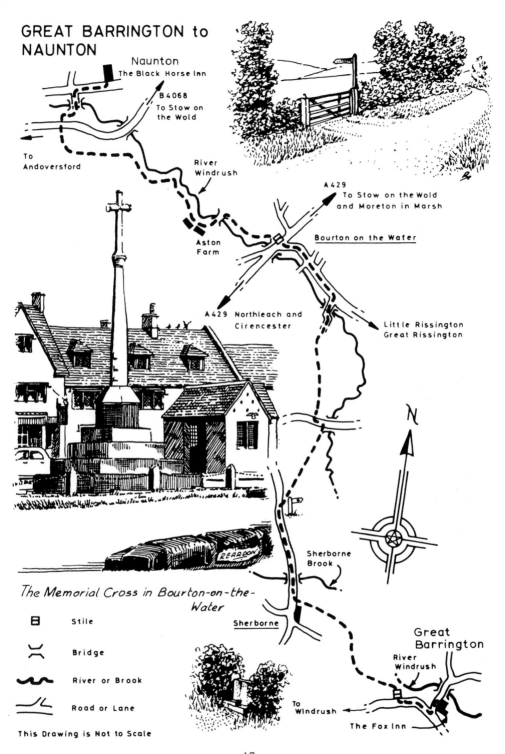

GREAT BARRINGTON to NAUNTON

Naunton
The Black Horse Inn

B4068
To Stow on the Wold

To Andoversford

River Windrush

A429
To Stow on the Wold and Moreton in Marsh

Aston Farm

Bourton on the Water

A429 Northleach and Cirencester

Little Rissington
Great Rissington

N

Sherborne Brook

Sherborne

Great Barrington

River Windrush

To Windrush

The Fox Inn

The Memorial Cross in Bourton-on-the-Water

Symbol	Description
⊟	Stile
⏝	Bridge
〰	River or Brook
╱	Road or Lane

This Drawing is Not to Scale

17

The path soon meets the B4068 road where you turn right. After about 100 yards turn left on a well marked Bridleway which drops steeply down to the delightful Cotswold village of Naunton. Cross the fast flowing River Windrush where you emerge on a metalled road almost opposite your next port of call, The Black Horse Inn.

Built of golden Cotswold stone in the traditional style of the 17th century, the Inn serves good food and beers in peaceful surroundings. The building was originally two cottages which housed farm workers and has beautifully exposed authentic beams to set off its tap room. An Inn for a most relaxing rest.

'The Old Mill' viewed from the road bridge in Naunton.

The Black Horse Inn, Naunton.

The Farmers Arms, Guiting Power.

The Black Horse Inn, Naunton to
The Farmer's Arms, Guiting Power

Distance 2 miles

Prepare yourself for two splendid short sections from Naunton to Guiting Power and on to Kineton. If you had to choose three and a half miles of Gloucestershire to sum up The Cotswolds, these could well be your first choice.

Leave The Black Horse Inn and turn right to make your way through the village, lined with warm limestone houses. You will spot staddle stones and mill wheels and even a dovecote as you climb towards the B4068 and pass St. Andrew's Church.

Climb towards the Cheltenham Road and just before meeting the B road take a well signed footpath to your right marked Wardens' Way. Now follow the Yellow Arrows. After a short field section, the path joins an unclassified road, where you turn right and drop down to a T junction.

Your footpath to Guiting Power is directly opposite the junction and is well marked. It passes the quiet little wetland that is the Guiting Power Nature Reserve before winding its way to emerge to the left of St Michael's Church. A very short road walk now takes you into the heart of the village which you will find is almost forgotten by the passing of time.

At the picturesque village green, turn right and make your way to your next stop, The Farmer's Arms Inn. The Inn boasts a fine example of an English skittle alley and large function room both well used by visitors and locals alike. Once again, the exposed beams and original stone slabs inside add to the traditional welcome that this pub offers. Here too is another opportunity to obtain good food and excellent beer.

The old village pump, still to be seen on the North side of the main road through the village of Naunton.

The Dove-cote in Naunton is all that remains of a once fine Manor House that was close by. This Dove-cote, built in the 16th century has over 1000 nest-holes. Pigeon meat was very popular in those days, especially during the winter months with the wealthy landowners.

NAUNTON to GUITING POWER

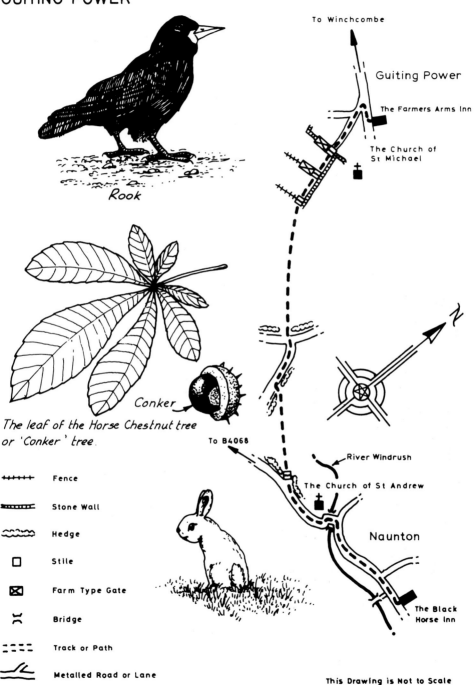

Rook

Conker

The leaf of the Horse Chestnut tree
or 'Conker' tree.

To Winchcombe

Guiting Power

The Farmers Arms Inn

The Church of
St Michael

To B4068

River Windrush

The Church of St Andrew

Naunton

The Black
Horse Inn

++++++   Fence

▰▰▰▰▰   Stone Wall

〰〰〰   Hedge

▢   Stile

⊠   Farm Type Gate

⏝   Bridge

- - - -   Track or Path

〜   Metalled Road or Lane

This Drawing is Not to Scale

21

The Farmer's Arms Inn, Guiting Power to
The Half Way House Inn, Kineton

Distance 1¹/₂ miles

Leave The Farmer's Arms Inn and turn right to walk back through the village to pass the village green on your left. Now look once again for the Wardens' Way on your right and follow it through the cottages, out of the village and down to the River Windrush.

Where the path meets the river, it divides. Leave the Wardens' Way and follow the path over the river and off to your left. After a short climb out of the valley, the path leads you onto the Barton Road where you turn left.

Continue on and then turn right after the 1st house on your right. Take the time to gaze to your left as you climb the first field. A magnificent sight awaits you, featuring the local Manor House set against the splendour of Guiting Wood.

You soon enter Kineton by the corrugated sheds of Home Farm. Turn left for your next stop at The Half Way House Inn. This Inn is truly old and once belonged to Corpus Christi College, Oxford.

Whichever season you decide to visit, you will not be disappointed. In the warm summer evenings, the Inn offers the use of its large, pleasant garden and in the winter features real log fires. Once again, the menu is extensive, offering home made soups in the winter and homemade pies throughout the year to complement the Donnington beers.

Yellow Arrows on
Marker Posts

Yellow Arrow on
Tree

Yellow Arrows on Farm
buildings and Telegraph
poles.

Waymarker Post indicating
a Bridleway. A similar post
indicates a Footpath.

Showing You the Way

GUITING POWER to KINETON

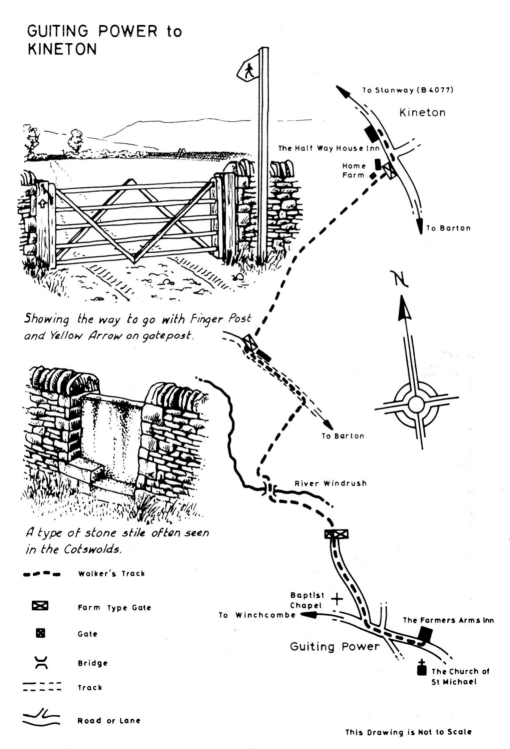

Showing the way to go with Finger Post and Yellow Arrow on gatepost.

A type of stone stile often seen in the Cotswolds.

To Stanway (B 4077)

Kineton

The Half Way House Inn

Home Farm

To Barton

N

To Barton

River Windrush

Baptist Chapel

To Winchcombe

The Farmers Arms Inn

Guiting Power

The Church of St Michael

- - - Walker's Track

Farm Type Gate

Gate

Bridge

- - - Track

Road or Lane

This Drawing is Not to Scale

The Half Way House Inn, Kineton to
The Plough Inn, Ford

Distance 2 miles

This section starts off badly due to the lack of an accessible footpath and a long road section to walk, but ends in style.

Leave The Half Way House Inn and turn right out of the village. Now follow this unclassified road for a full mile to Temple Guiting. At the school, turn right and drop down into the village.

Immediately after Manor Farm look for a footpath sign on your left which takes you up a small lane. Here a great surprise may await you, as you will now pass by the only Llama farm in The Cotswolds. This lane soon runs into a small field where you continue straight ahead. After 200 yards, a footpath goes left down to the valley bottom but ignore the sign and continue ahead.

After 200 yards the track sweeps right, and here you leave it and follow a footpath taking you left towards the B4077. Just before the end of the second field the footpath goes left and soon pops out onto the B road where you turn left.

Your journey now becomes potentially dangerous as you have no choice but to walk alongside the busy road for 200 yards. Soon your next stop is found on a bend in the road, the ancient Plough Inn.

The Inn is one of England's oldest and was used as a Court House in days gone by. Authentic throughout, you cannot fail to be left breathless by the sheer beauty of blackened beams set in Cotswold stone. Historical features of interest include two vast fireplaces, handmade hinges in the doors, the "Bars up" ancient door securing device and the remains of the stocks in one bar.

The pub is particularly popular with foreign visitors, many of whom would like to take the entire building home. Once again, The Plough Inn serves fine beers and an extensive menu renowned across The Cotswolds for its fresh asparagus dishes when in season.

Weeping Willow

Water Shrew

Great Spearwort

Water Crowfoot

KINETON to FORD

Magpie

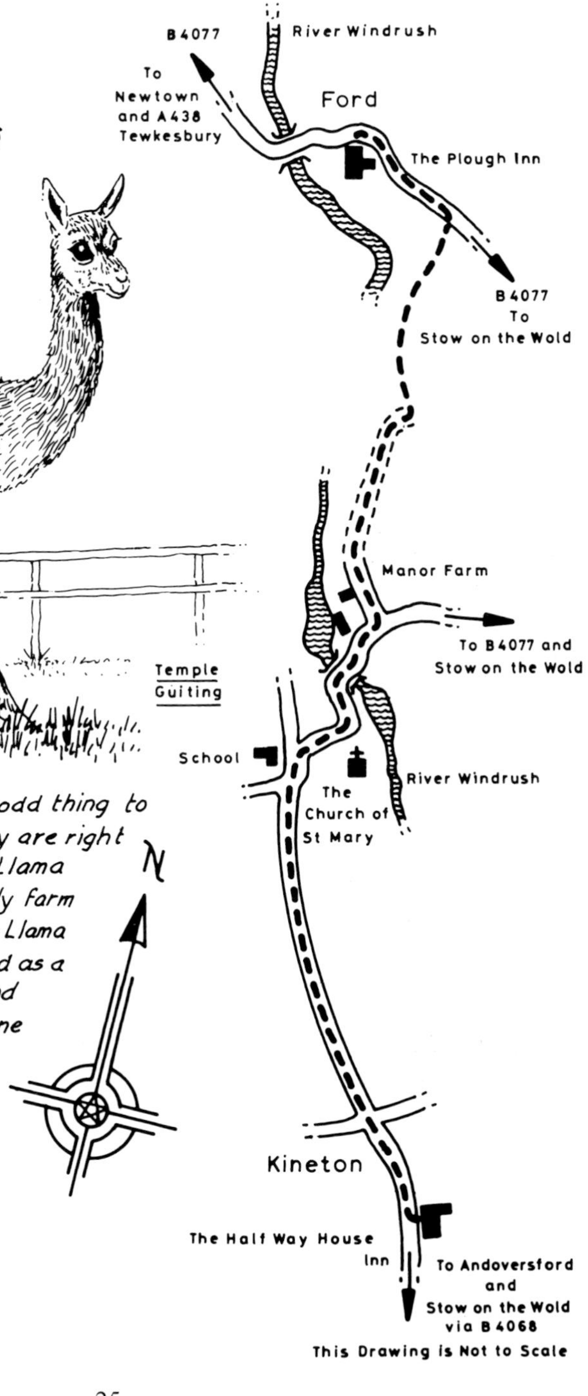

The sketch shows a Llama, an odd thing to find in the Cotswolds, but they are right there. They can be seen in the Llama Farm in Temple Guiting, the only farm of its kind in the Cotswolds. The Llama comes from S America and is used as a 'beast of burden' in the Andes and South American countries. The one shown is the Llama Guanaco.

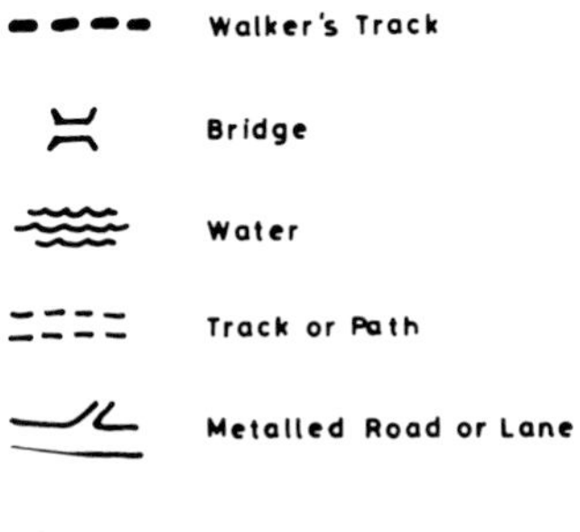

- - - - Walker's Track

⊃⊂ Bridge

≋ Water

= = = = Track or Path

⌒ Metalled Road or Lane

B 4077   River Windrush

To Newtown and A438 Tewkesbury

Ford

The Plough Inn

B 4077 To Stow on the Wold

Manor Farm

To B 4077 and Stow on the Wold

Temple Guiting

School

The Church of St Mary

River Windrush

N

Kineton

The Half Way House Inn

To Andoversford and Stow on the Wold via B 4068

This Drawing is Not to Scale

The Half Way House Inn, Kineton.

The Plough Inn, Ford.

The Snowshill Arms, Snowshill.

The Church and Post Office in the famous village of Snowshill, in the Cotswolds of Gloucestershire.

PEARSON

The Plough Inn, Ford to
The Snowshill Arms, Snowshill

Distance 3 miles

Yet another super section awaits! Leave The Plough Inn and cross the busy B4077 and take the footpath directly opposite. After 100 yards the path divides and you follow the Yellow Arrow to the left. After a further 200 yards the path again divides and you turn right. The path is easily followed with a series of well kept stiles and Yellow Arrow markings. Very soon you emerge onto a metalled road in the hamlet of Cutsdean and keep the church on your left.

Cross the road and pick up a footpath opposite for Taddington, leaving Cutsdean alongside the picturesque Post Office. Follow the arrrows which after 300 yards takes you left and through a valley.

Once again, the footpath meets a small unclassified road with farm buildings on your right. Turn right and follow the road for one and a quarter miles to a Y junction.

At this junction, there is a footpath going left alongside the wood, ignore it and take a bridleway heading slightly right. It crosses two fields before once again meeting a small metalled road. Turn right and follow the road into the village of Snowshill and onto your next stop, The Snowshill Arms.

Snowshill village is a photographer's delight, built as it is around the church, and featuring an old Manor House now owned and preserved by The National Trust.

The Manor is a charming Tudor building with a "William and Mary" front. Toys, musical instruments, spinners and weavers' tools, clocks and bicycles pack the house from ground floor to attic and make it a treasure that must not be missed. Its pleasant, attractive terraced gardens overlook farmlands lying in the Avon Valley and Midland Plain.

Like its neighbour, The Manor, The Snowshill Arms is old and retains all the qualities of a real English Inn. Parts of it date back to the 13th century and its features include exposed beams and an array of farm implements around the bar. Until the 1900s, landlords brewed their own beer here. Today, a range of Donnington beers are on offer to accompany a full menu of bar snacks for the hungry walker.

Two popular attractions at The Snowshill Arms are the well-used skittle alley and the extensive rear gardens full of adventure climbs to entertain the many young visitors during the summer months.

SNOWSHILL, A CHARMING and WELL KNOWN VILLAGE OF THE COTSWOLDS

28

FORD to SNOWSHILL

To Broadway

Snowshill Manor (N.T.)

The Snowshill Arms

Snowshill

The Church of St Barnabas

One of the interesting little figures to be found at Snowshill Manor, now in National Trust care.

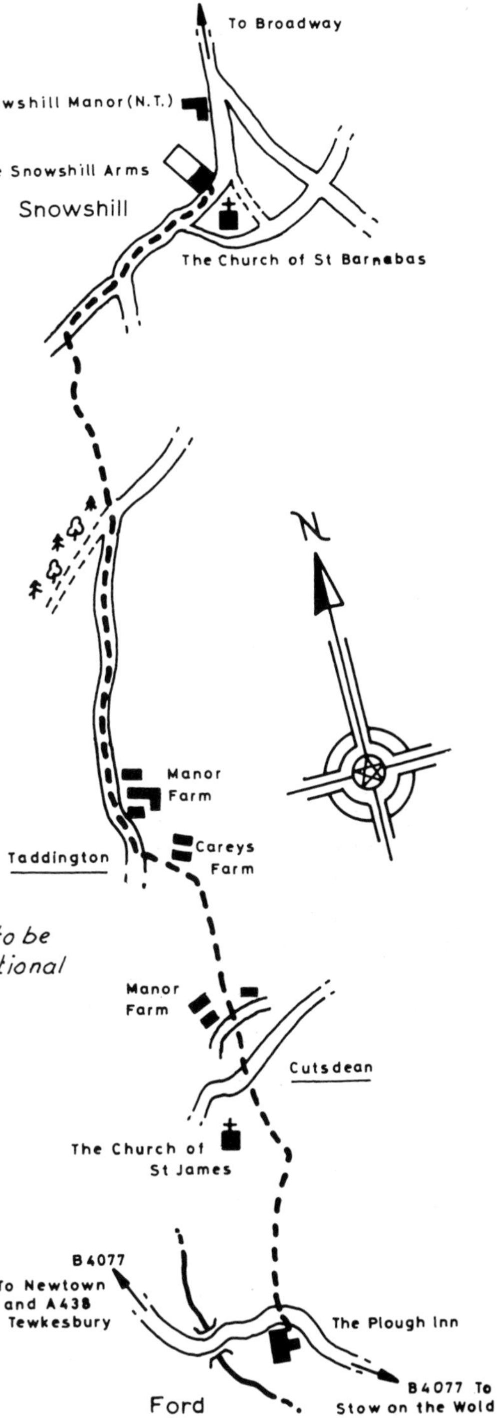

Manor Farm

Careys Farm

Taddington

Manor Farm

Cutsdean

The Church of St James

B 4077
To Newtown
and A438
Tewkesbury

The Plough Inn

B 4077 To
Stow on the Wold

Ford

- - - - Walker's Track

◲ Indicates Presence of Farm
Farm

~~~ River or Stream

≍ Bridge

:⊐⊐⊐⊐ Track or Footpath

⌣⌣ Metalled Road or Lane

This Drawing is Not to Scale

29

The Snowshill Arms, Snowshill to
The Mount Inn, Stanton

Keep your camera at hand as the next two sections will keep you busy. Both Snowshill and Stanton largely remain unspoilt examples of what The Cotswolds are all about and caught in sunlight are sights to live forever in your memory.

Leave The Snowshill Arms and make your way back out of the village in the same direction as you entered. Take the first turning right marked with a "No Through Road" sign and very soon go right again at a T junction. Walk down the road for about 200 yards and look for a Yellow Arrowed footpath sign on a gate on your left. This path takes you up a field into Littleworth Wood.

The path is little used but very soon meets a better used track where you bear left in the centre of the wood. Continue left through the wood until once again meeting a small metalled road where you turn right.

Now take great care not to divert from this road as it soon crosses the Cotswold Way. Continue straight ahead on what now becomes a dirt track through a metal gate.

The downhill walk now offers superb panoramic views of Winchcombe, Cleeve Hill, Bredon Hill and in the distance the Malvern Hills. This track now takes you direct to your next stop, The Mount Inn.

Again, a lovely unspoilt Inn offering fine views from its bar and gardens. The interior boasts a comprehensive collection of horse brasses and leathers which in the winter months can be admired in the flickering light of a real log fire.

This popular Inn maintains an extensive menu throughout the year, including homemade soups and a speciality dish of "Cow Pie". Summer visitors can join in with the garden game of "boules" which has become very popular with the locals, who also represent the pub in friendly cricket matches under the name "MCC".

The drawing shows an old Wellhead which at one time covered the spring – the original water supply of the Manor – which may be found in the terraced gardens of Snowshill Manor, now National Trust Property and open to the Public.

SNOWSHILL to STANTON

To A46 and
Winchcombe

To A46 and
Broadway

Stanton

The Church of
St Michael

The Mount Inn

DELIGHTFUL COTSWOLD COTTAGES
at STANTON, GLOS

REARDON

Littleworth Wood

Magpie

The
Snowshill Arms

Snowshill Manor (N.T.)

Church of
St Barnabas

Snowshill

To
Broadway

- - - - - Trackway or Path

〜〜 Road or Lane

This Drawing is Not to Scale

31

The Mount Inn, Stanton to
The New Inn, Willersey

Distance 5 miles

Keep the camera at hand as you will need it a lot during this section. Stanton is one of the most picturesque villages in England and parts of Laverton, Buckland and Broadway on your journey to Willersey will make you green with envy.

Leave The Mount and make your way down through the village. Stanton is a village of true outstanding natural beauty which was tastefully restored by Sir Philip Stott in the early 1900s. The Jacobean House which was his home even outshines the 16th century manor house.

At the village Cross, turn right for the church with its perpendicular tower and spire and its porch with two levels. It is well worth a moment of your time to go into the church and wonder at its lovingly restored interior, including two pulpits and the remains of wall paintings in the north transept.

Your way now follows a well-marked footpath which goes through the churchyard and runs around to the right of the church. At the stile, there is a choice of three footpaths and you should take the one going left for Laverton.

You are now walking parallel with the main road but would hardly know it as it seems you are in the heart of the countryside. After four fields you join a metalled road and turn right to loop your way around Laverton.

Your route takes you past tastefully renovated cottages and a small village green. Opposite is a "Telephone Kiosk" sign alongside a bridleway. Take the bridleway which soon takes you to Buckland.

This is a delightful village with a fascinating church containing 15th century glass and 17th century seating and pulpit. Buckland Rectory is one of the oldest medieval parsonages in the country and dates back to the 15th century.

On entering Buckland, turn right and walk up the sparsely built main road and past picture postcard houses and The Country House Hotel.

Follow the road past Buckland Court on your right. Here the barns and outbuildings have been tastefully converted into holiday accommodation. As the road climbs right, look for a Yellow Arrowed footpath sign in the left hand corner of "Hillside Cottage" and "The Bothy".

The path leads to a stile which you cross and turn left. The footpath should now be followed on your map and takes you around the wood, steadily climbing before it eventually joins The Cotswold Way and drops down to The West End. The well-used footpath now takes you into the tourist haunt of Broadway.

Wide streets, bordered with trim greens and 17th and 18th century houses make up Broadway which is, without doubt, one of England's show villages. Broadway retains a high degree of charm and beauty and offers a number of interesting shops and tea rooms.

Walk through the main street of Broadway and eventually turn left on the B4632 Leamington Road. Take the last estate road on your right into Sandscroft Avenue and follow the estate round for about 300 yards. Alongside No 35 is a footpath marked with Yellow Arrows which twists its way across several fields (and a new and busy By-Pass which should be crossed with care) before emerging on the driveway for Warners Farm. Turn left down the driveway onto the B4632 where you turn right.

The road now takes you directly into Willersey and your next stop, The New Inn. Once again, in the tradition of Donnington Inns, The New Inn has its origins stretching back more than 300 to 400 years. One feature is its skittle alley and function room which is well-used by locals and visitors alike. A range of pub games are on offer as well as good food and excellent beer.

STANTON to WILLERSEY

The famous Broadway Tower built
in 1800 by the Earl of Coventry for
his Countess.

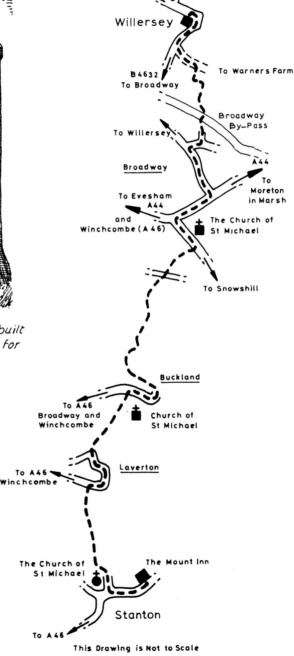

To Stratford upon Avon
B4632

St Peter's Church

Willersey

B4632
To Broadway

To Warners Farm

Broadway
By-Pass

To Willersey

A44

Broadway

To Moreton
in Marsh

To Evesham
A44

and
Winchcombe (A46)

The Church of
St Michael

To Snowshill

Buckland

To A46
Broadway and
Winchcombe

Church of
St Michael

To A46
Winchcombe

Laverton

The Church of
St Michael

The Mount Inn

Stanton

To A46

N

- ● ● ● ● Walker's Track
- - - - - - Driveway or Track
- ～⌐⌐ Road or Lane

This Drawing is Not to Scale

33

The New Inn, Willersey to
The Black Bear Inn, Moreton-in-Marsh   Distance 9¹/₄ miles

Your route between Willersey and Moreton-in-Marsh takes in yet more Cotswold treasures, including Chipping Campden, Broad Campden and Blockley.

Leave The New Inn and walk down the B4632 to one of the finest village ponds in England. Turn right into Church Street and make your way up the road to St Peter's Church. Here you pick up a footpath running left through the graveyard where the path divides and you take the right hand one. Cross the stream on a stone bridge and take the left hand path. Cross a second stream almost immediately and keep to the right. After 30 yards, turn right and head for the church with a very pointed spire on the hill. This is St Nicholas's Church at Saintbury and well worth a visit, containing as it does a 15th century font and 18th century cover, looking over equally old box pews.

From the lower churchyard gate, walk down towards the village. When the shore lane joins a road turn right and walk back up the road for about 20 yards before taking a footpath on your left. Follow the Yellow Arrowed route.

After a pleasant walk, the path crosses a bridleway. Ignore the bridleway signs and continue straight ahead on the footpath.

After 30 yards, cross the stream on a wooden bridge. At this point the path divides three ways but you continue straight ahead and climb the hill. The path eventually comes out onto a minor road where you turn right and follow the road uphill.

After a short distance, at a National Trust sign for Dovers Hill, turn left through a kissing gate and climb to a topograph to your right. Here is a magnificent view of the surrounding countryside.

Dovers Hill is the site of the famous Cotswold Games, founded during the reign of James I by Captain Robert Dover. They continue today, although their history is chequered due to their suppression during the Cromwellian period and in later years the behaviour of riotous Irish navvies in 1851 who, no doubt, would have revelled in the favourite Cotswold "game" of shin-kicking.

Now walk to the right for about 300 yards, around the escarpment. Here a Yellow Arrow with a white dot on it takes you right and down into the ever popular town of Chipping Campden. Your walk into Campden may well whet your appetite to next walk the Cotswold Way which is a fine, long distance walk which starts in the town.

Chipping Campden is arguably the finest of the Cotswold wool towns and it was at the height of its prosperity in the late Middle Ages. It has aged with grace and while catering for the tourist has not lowered its standards to pander to them.

At St Catherine's Church turn left and first right into Sheep Street. The route you are now about to take leads you out of Campden but a diversion into the town is well worth taking. Of the many architectural delights on offer, there are gems in the form of Grevel's House, Bedfont House and the charming little Woolstaplers' Hall Museum.

After 300 yards of Sheep Street, turn left on an unclassified road to Broad Campden. Wind your way through this affluent village and climb a small rise of the road. Just past a house named "The Farthings" turn right onto a public footpath. This climbs steeply up a field before rejoining the unclassified road to Blockley. Cross straight over and turn right in the woods on a path which runs parallel to the road.

When the path meets an estate road, turn right and back up to the road. Here turn left. Approximately 300 yards past Hangman's Hall Farm, as the road sweeps left, turn right and climb up a well-marked bridleway. At the top of the rise, the bridleway doubles back to the right and you go left on a Yellowed Arrowed footpath soon dropping into a valley.

A steady climb uphill eventually brings you to a flatter, grassy area. Now consult your map to find an unmarked path which runs straight ahead across a field and into the houses of Blockley. Turn left down Greenway Road and right into Park Road.

WILLERSEY to
MORETON in MARSH

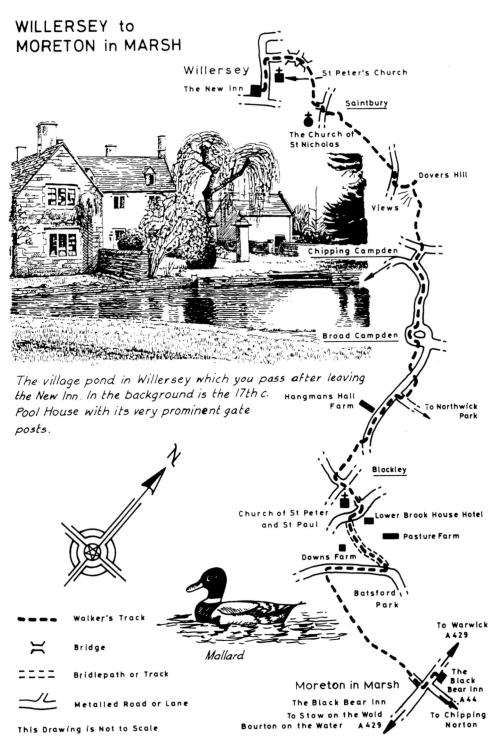

Willersey

The New Inn

St Peter's Church

Saintbury

The Church of
St Nicholas

Dovers Hill

Views

Chipping Campden

Broad Campden

The village pond in Willersey which you pass after leaving the New Inn. In the background is the 17th c. Pool House with its very prominent gate posts.

Hangmans Hall
Farm

To Northwick
Park

Blockley

Church of St Peter
and St Paul

Lower Brook House Hotel

Pasture Farm

Downs Farm

Batsford
Park

To Warwick
A 429

Mallard

- - - Walker's Track

)(Bridge

= = = = Bridlepath or Track

⌐⌐ Metalled Road or Lane

This Drawing is Not to Scale

Moreton in Marsh

The Black Bear Inn
To Stow on the Wold
Bourton on the Water   A 429

The
Black
Bear Inn
A 44

To Chipping
Norton

Blockley is a mysterious village and delights the visitor with steep streets of character terraces, full of 17th, 18th and 19th century buildings. Owing much of its prosperity to the silk trade, Blockley once boasted six mills employing more than 500 people.

Turn left into the parish churchyard and take time out to visit the church with its Norman chancel. Go left again in front of the church and drop down to the B4479 road where you turn right.

Just past Lower Brook House, turn left on a bridleway marked Pasture Farm. At the top of the rise take the Blue Arrowed bridleway to the right of a large barn. Follow the bridleway around the escarpment until it joins several divided ways.

Turn right on a footpath, keeping Downs Farm on your right. Eventually, the path comes out on a small unclassified road where you turn right.

You now have a large estate wall on your left which you make your way along and around. After approximately a quarter of a mile, the wall goes left and you follow it on a footpath around the estate downhill to eventually pass two gate houses.

At the end of the estate wall, the path divides and you should keep straight ahead. This well-used path now takes you across several fields and kissing gates to emerge in Moreton-in-Marsh.

On reaching the houses, walk straight ahead for the Market Place and your next stop, The Black Bear Inn. This is reputed to be haunted by a ghost called 'Fred' who has been known to play tricks on customers.

The Inn, which is large and recently renovated, features an unusual collection of 19th century photographs of Moreton-in-Marsh and surrounding areas. It offers accommodation, fine food and of course yet another chance to sample a wide range of Donnington ales.

Moreton-in-Marsh is a popular centre for the tourist trade, lying as it does on the crossroads of several routes and being connected to London by rail.

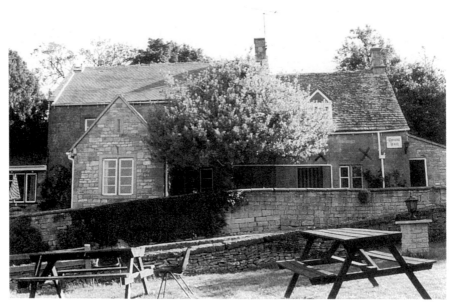

The Mount Inn, Stanton.

The New Inn, Willersey.

The Black Bear Inn, Moreton in Marsh.

The Black Bear Inn, Moreton-in-Marsh to
The Red Lion Inn, Little Compton

Distance 5¹/₄ miles

Leave the Black Bear Inn and take the busy A44 out of Moreton-in-Marsh for a full one and a half miles until you pass the Fire Service College. Take the unclassified road left marked Great Wolford at the "Four Shires Stone".

The stone is an impressive 18th century monument, topped by a sundial and a ball, marking the old boundaries of the counties of Gloucestershire, Warwickshire, Oxfordshire and Worcestershire. (N.B. The Worcestershire section has long been swallowed up into Gloucestershire).

Walk up the road for one third of a mile and turn right into a field on an unmarked footpath (second gate on the right). You now cross four fields until you arrive at a deer fence with a gate in it. Go through the gate and straight ahead through the break in the trees and another three deer fence gates. Now aim for the left side of the Manor House ahead of you. In the top left-hand corner of the field you join a dirt track and turn right into Barton-on-the-Heath. This village was once the home of Captain Robert Dover, the 17th century lawyer and founder of "The Cotswold Games".

At the road junction turn right again, marked Little Compton. Stay on this road through the village and past St Lawrence's Church. Approximately 20 yards after the church turn left onto a marked footpath and follow arrowed directions for the next one and a half miles.

Head for Salters Well Farm. At the farm pass the farm house on your right go through a gate, turn left and after a few yards turn right to follow the arrowed route downhill. The route eventually takes you right and almost directly to your next port of call, The Red Lion Inn in Little Compton, Warwickshire's most southerly village.

The Inn was built in the 16th century and boasts a fine lounge/restaurant and an exceptionally pretty garden. Approved by The Tourist Board and Egon Ronay it also features in the Good Beer Guide. The Red Lion serves wonderful meals, including a house speciality of rump steak cut to your liking. At the time of writing, the "record" steak to be served weighed in at a mighty 56ozs.

There is accommodation for up to six available, including a honeymoon suite. Here too is a fine collection of Donnington ales.

The Duck Pond
Moreton in Marsh

MORETON in MARSH to LITTLE COMPTON

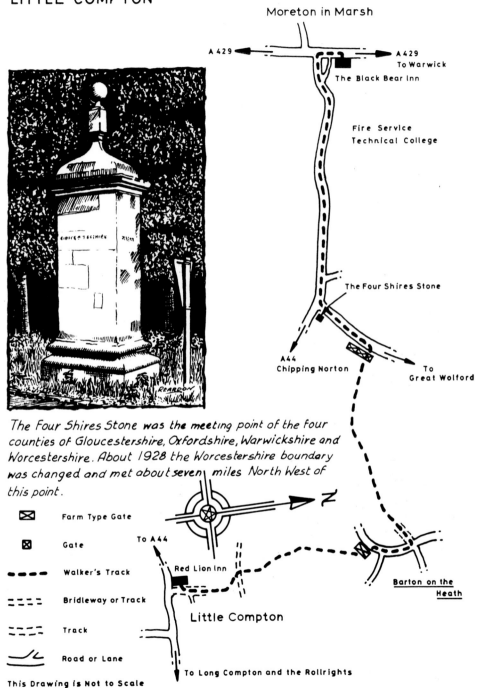

The Four Shires Stone was the meeting point of the four counties of Gloucestershire, Oxfordshire, Warwickshire and Worcestershire. About 1928 the Worcestershire boundary was changed and met about seven miles North West of this point.

⊠	Farm Type Gate
⊠	Gate
●━ ━ ━	Walker's Track
⌐ ⌐ ⌐ ⌐	Bridleway or Track
⌐ ⌐ ⌐ ⌐	Track
⌐⌐	Road or Lane

This Drawing is Not to Scale

The Red Lion Inn, Little Compton to
The Fox Inn, Broadwell

Distance 4¹/₂ miles

This section proved to be the most difficult to piece together without resorting to roads to join the villages of Evenlode and Broadwell. However, the effort is rewarded as you will find Broadwell to be a true delight.

Leave The Red Lion and cross over the road behind the car park. Look to your left and you will find a well-signed footpath taking you around a small field to the busy A44 road. Cross straight over and join an unclassified road for Chastleton.

After a quarter of a mile, turn left onto a signed footpath which eventually takes you over two stiles to emerge alongside Chastleton Church and its once magnificent Manor House. It was built by a local wool merchant, Walter Jones.

Turn left at the church and follow the road uphill for a quarter of mile where you turn right on to a well-signed bridleway. Your route now passes through Peasewell Wood and continues straight ahead to drop down to Horn Farm before joining a metalled road taking you into the village of Evenlode.

At the road junction turn left. There unfortunately is no alternative now but to use roads for the next one and a half miles. Follow the minor roads which now take you left out of Evenlode and then right towards Broadwell. This road will lead you straight into the heart of the village. At the end of Chapel Street turn right for the Village Green and your next stop, The Fox Inn.

Broadwell is a spacious village whose church stands in a tree-shaded churchyard and features several dignified 17th century table tombs. Here too is a monument dedicated to Herbert Weston and his wife, kneeling at a prayer desk.

The Fox Inn is traditionally built in Cotswold stone facing the spacious Green which itself is a popular venue for picnickers and touring groups of Morris Men. Inside is a collection of farm implements, adding to the real "village" atmosphere. The Inn offers an extensive menu, including a selection of homemade dishes and a range of Donnington beers. This is the 15th and final Inn on your tour. However, to get back to your starting point and complete the circle you now have a second opportunity to visit The Queen's Head Inn at Stow-on-the-Wold.

The popular wooden stile.

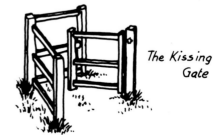

The 'Farm Type' Gate.

Gate found on
Walker's
footpath

The Kissing
Gate

LITTLE COMPTON to BROADWELL

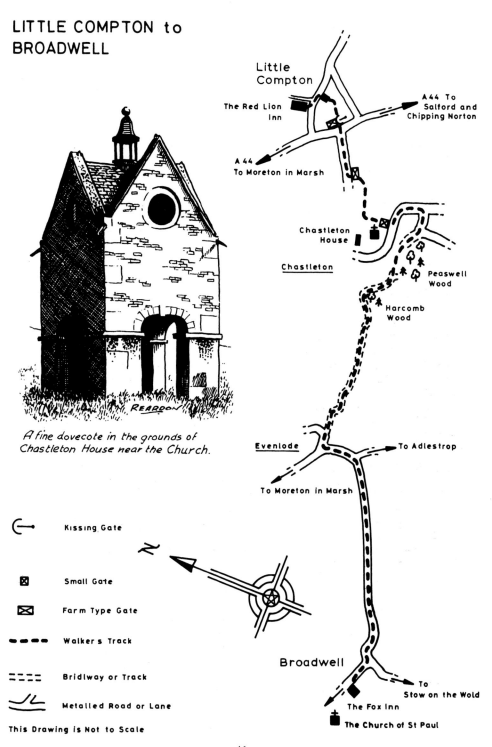

A fine dovecote in the grounds of Chastleton House near the Church.

Little Compton

The Red Lion Inn

A44 To Salford and Chipping Norton

A44 To Moreton in Marsh

Chastleton House

Chastleton

Peaswell Wood

Harcomb Wood

Evenlode

To Adlestrop

To Moreton in Marsh

Broadwell

To Stow on the Wold

The Fox Inn

The Church of St Paul

N

Kissing Gate

Small Gate

Farm Type Gate

Walkers Track

Bridlway or Track

Metalled Road or Lane

This Drawing is Not to Scale

41

The Fox Inn, Broadwell to
The Queen's Head Inn, Stow-on-the-Wold

Distance 1¹/₂ miles

From The Fox Inn, walk back down the Green and turn right on the road to Stow-on-the-Wold. Follow the road uphill and after about 300 yards turn left on a well-marked and well-used bridleway which takes you directly into Stow-on-the-Wold and The Queen's Head Inn.

The old Stocks on the Green in the Square in Stow on the Wold.

The famous old well known as "The Wells". Believed to be about 2000 years old, the water from the spring is crystal clear.

BROADWELL to
STOW on the WOLD

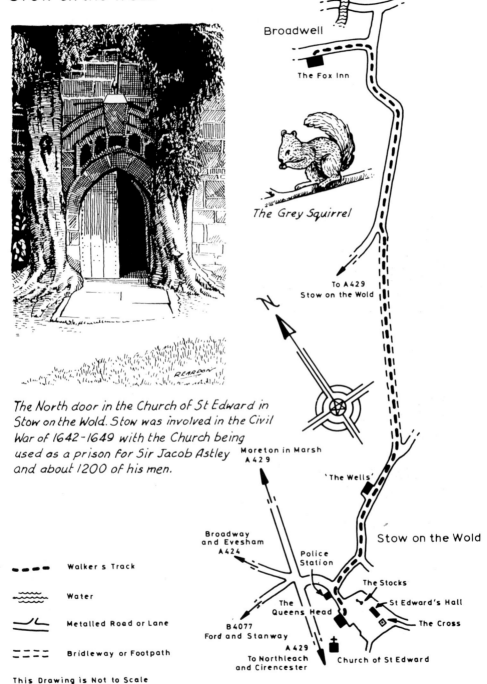

The North door in the Church of St Edward in
Stow on the Wold. Stow was involved in the Civil
War of 1642-1649 with the Church being
used as a prison for Sir Jacob Astley
and about 1200 of his men.

Ford

Broadwell

The Fox Inn

The Grey Squirrel

To A429
Stow on the Wold

N

Moreton in Marsh
A429

'The Wells'

Stow on the Wold

Broadway
and Evesham
A424

Police
Station

The Stocks

The
Queens Head

St Edward's Hall

B4077
Ford and Stanway

The Cross

A429
To Northleach
and Cirencester

Church of St Edward

- - - - Walker's Track

~~~~ Water

⌐⌐ Metalled Road or Lane

= = = = Bridleway or Footpath

This Drawing is Not to Scale

The Red Lion, Little Compton.

The Fox Inn, Broadwell.